THE STORY OF THE
DETROIT

PISTONS

CREATIVE ◖ EDUCATION

Published by Creative Education
123 South Broad Street
Mankato, Minnesota 56001
Creative Education is an imprint of The Creative Company.

DESIGN AND PRODUCTION BY **EVANSDAY DESIGN**

PHOTOGRAPHS BY Getty Images (Glen Allison, Bill Baptist /
NBAE, Nathaniel S. Butler, Allen Einstein / NBAE, Focus on
Sport, Jesse D. Garrabrant / NBAE, Otto Greule Jr. / Allsport,
Andy Hayt / NBAE, Kent Horner / NBAE, Keystone Features,
D. Lippitt / Einstein / NBAE, Joe Patronite / Allsport, Tom
Pidgeon, Ezra Shaw, Jerry Wachter / NBAE)

LIBRARY OF CONGRESS CATALOGING-IN-PUBLICATION DATA

LeBoutillier, Nate.
The story of the Detroit Pistons / by Nate LeBoutillier.
p. cm. — (The NBA—a history of hoops)
ISBN-13: 978-1-58341-406-4
1. Detroit Pistons (Basketball team)—History—
Juvenile literature. I. Title. II. Series.

GV885.52.D47L43 2006
796.323'64'0979461—dc22 2005051203

First edition

9 8 7 6 5 4 3 2 1

COVER PHOTO: *Chauncey Billups*

THE STORY OF THE
DETROIT
PISTONS

NATE LeBOUTILLIER

CREATIVE ✦ EDUCATION

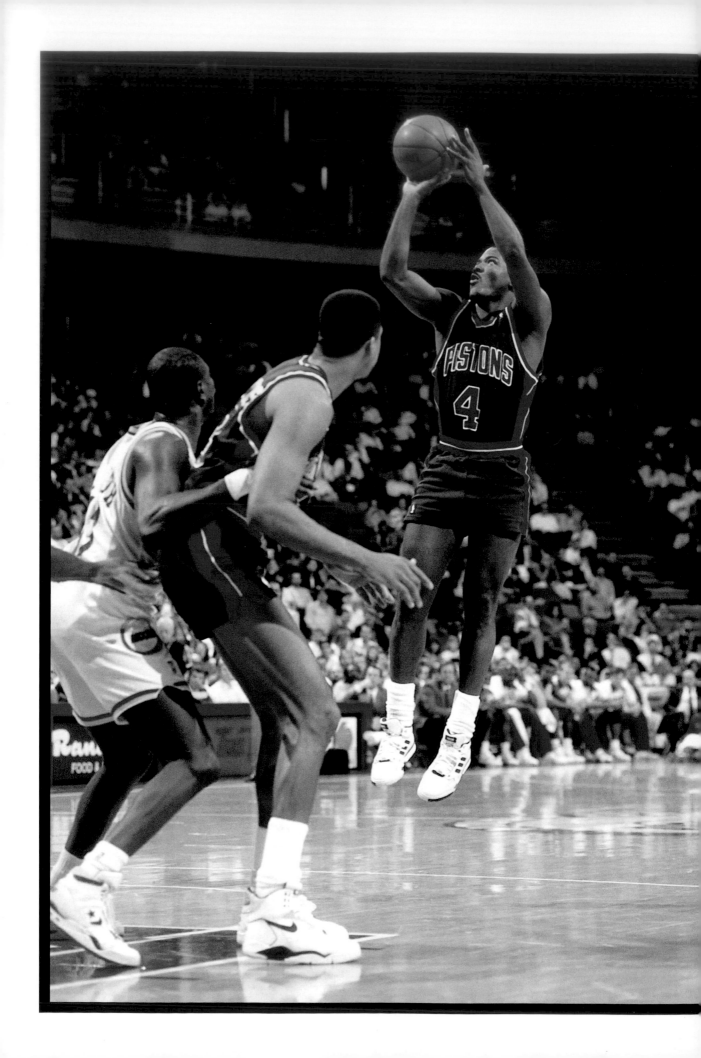

Isiah Thomas

HURLING HIS 6-FOOT-1 BODY LIKE A DART TOWARD THE BASKET THROUGH DEFENSIVE GIANTS SEEMINGLY TWICE HIS SIZE. JOE DUMARS ATTACHING HIMSELF ON DEFENSE LIKE A POSTAGE STAMP TO THE MAN HE GUARDED. BILL LAIMBEER DIGGING INTO OPPONENTS' RIBCAGES WITH HIS SHARP ELBOWS. RICK MAHORN BUMPING HIPS WITH ANY WHO DARED IMPEDE HIS PATH. DENNIS RODMAN SPRINGING FOR REBOUNDS LIKE HE WAS ON A TRAMPOLINE. VINNIE "THE MICRO-WAVE" JOHNSON PUMPING IN JUMP SHOT AFTER JUMP SHOT IN ASSEMBLY LINE-LIKE FASHION. THE '80S WERE TURNING INTO THE '90S, AND THE DETROIT PISTONS WERE REVVING HIGH.

DETROIT PISTONS
Detroit Michigan

GETTING THE PISTONS PUMPING

DETROIT, MICHIGAN, STARTED OUT AS A TINY FRENCH

fort in 1701. It became such a key site for fur trading

that French and British armies and Native American

bands fought many battles to gain control of it over

the years. Today, Detroit is known as the "Motor City"

because it is the home of American car manufactur-

ers Ford, General Motors, and Chrysler. Since 1957, the

city has hosted a National Basketball Association (NBA)

team. Given Detroit's business in building cars and car

parts, it was only fitting that that franchise was named

the Pistons.

The Pistons franchise actually started out in Fort Wayne,

Indiana, in 1937. The team played in a small, industrial

league under the ownership of Fred Zollner. In 1941,

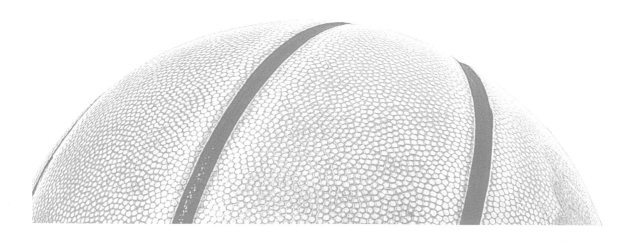

9

PX
DONUT
SHOPS

The "Pistons" name is a fitting one, as illustrated by this 1946 photograph of a busy "Motor City" street

Few NBA players worked harder than Dave DeBusschere, a Detroit native known for his tenacious defense

the Pistons joined the National Basketball League (NBL), one of the first professional leagues. Fort Wayne soon dominated the NBL, winning the league championship in 1944 and 1945 behind the leadership of star guard Bobby McDermott. In 1949, the Pistons joined the NBA.

In 1954, Zollner hired Charlie Eckman—a former NBA referee—as the Pistons' new head coach. Eckman guided a talented team starring forward George Yardley, and the Pistons were the NBA Finals runner-up in both 1954–55 and 1955–56. The fans in Fort Wayne loved their team, but Zollner didn't think that the Pistons could compete for long in such a small city. So, the Pistons said good-bye to Fort Wayne and moved to Detroit in 1957.

The move seemed to hurt the team, which posted losing records year after year in Detroit. Young swingman Dave DeBusschere and a guard named Dave Bing were the lone bright spots. As a rookie in 1966–67, Bing scored 20 points per game and was named NBA Rookie of the Year. "You can't open up a man's chest and look at his heart," said legendary Boston Celtics coach Red Auerbach. "But I guarantee there's one big [heart] beating in Bing. Give me one man like Dave Bing, and I'll build a championship team around him."

Unfortunately, the Pistons were never able to do that. The team made the playoffs after the 1967–68 season but struggled the next year after trading DeBusschere to the New York Knicks. DeBusschere went on to help the Knicks capture two NBA championships, while the Pistons sank to the bottom of the league standings again.

LANIER DRIVES DETROIT

WITH THE FIRST PICK IN THE 1970 NBA DRAFT, Detroit selected a young center named Bob Lanier. At 6-foot-11 and a muscular 275 pounds, Lanier relied on power. "I was well aware of Bob's great strength," said Cleveland Cavaliers center Steve Patterson after battling Lanier for a rebound. "I hammered him, and I practically hung on him. Then, all of a sudden,… he just wrapped his arm around me and threw me to the ground like I was made of straw.… I still don't know how he did it."

PISTONS

Bob Lanier was known for his graceful hook shot, big feet (he wore size 22 shoes), and remarkable power

14

Isiah Thomas was one of basketball's friendliest stars off the court but a cold-blooded competitor on it

In 1973–74, under new coach Ray Scott, Detroit jumped to a 52–30 mark and made the playoffs for the first of two straight seasons. But those would be the Pistons' last good seasons for a long time. In 1976, Detroit bid farewell to Bing, trading him to the Washington Bullets. In 1979, the team dealt Lanier to the Milwaukee Bucks, and Detroit plunged to 16–66. The Pistons desperately needed a hero.

The 1981 NBA Draft provided the Pistons with that hero: point guard Isiah Thomas. Thomas had just led Indiana University to the national collegiate championship, and the Pistons believed that he could carry them to the top as well. "I believe God made people to perform certain acts," said Will Robinson, Detroit's assistant general manager. "Frank Sinatra was made to sing, Jesse Owens was made to run, and Isiah Thomas was made to play basketball."

Detroit hired Chuck Daly as its head coach in 1983. He guided a team on which Thomas controlled the ball, forward Kelly Tripucka led the team in scoring, and bruising center Bill Laimbeer banged the boards. Sharpshooting guards Joe Dumars and Vinnie Johnson, meanwhile, received few headlines but played steady roles. The Pistons were improving quickly.

THE MICROWAVE

Nicknames have always been a part of basketball. Sir Charles, Larry Legend, Magic, Pistol Pete, The Mailman, The Big Dipper, Dr. J, Thunder Dan, The Glove, The Pearl, The Dream, The Glide. On May 5, 1985, "The Microwave" was born. Scoring 22 of the Pistons' 26 final points in a 102–99 win over the Boston Celtics, reserve guard Vinnie Johnson wowed Pistons fans. Celtics guard Danny Ainge said afterwards, "If that guy in Chicago [football player William Perry] is 'The Refrigerator,' then Vinnie Johnson is 'The Microwave.' He sure heated up in a hurry." The Microwave, with the squat frame and muscles of a weightlifter, was most famous for hitting the Game 5, championship-clinching shot in the 1990 NBA Finals. His number 15 jersey was retired by the Pistons in 1994.

THE PISTONS OF THE MID-1980S CLEARLY HAD TALENT, but equally impressive was their hustling style of play. Coach Daly preached an aggressive defense, and the Pistons—nicknamed the "Bad Boys" for their physical style—often seemed like they had six or seven men on the floor. Usually guarding the opposing team's best offensive player was forward Dennis Rodman, who used his quick feet and wiry frame to become one of the NBA's best defenders.

17

PISTONS

Forward Dennis Rodman was arguably the best defender and rebounder in the NBA in the 1990s

BASKETBALL

A quiet and classy leader, Joe Dumars would become Detroit's general manager after his playing days ended

In 1986, Detroit traded Tripucka and added forward Adrian Dantley. The Pistons soared to 52–30 and reached the 1987 Eastern Conference Finals, where they fell to the Boston Celtics. In 1987–88, they made the NBA Finals, losing to the Los Angeles Lakers in seven tough games. The next season, Detroit would not be denied.

The Pistons went 63–19 and pounded their way through the playoffs to again meet the Lakers in the Finals. This time, the Pistons swept the Lakers in four games behind the hot shooting of Dumars. The versatile guard exploded for more than 27 points per game during the series. "Dumars wouldn't miss," said Mitch Kupchak, a Lakers team official. "We kept waiting for him to miss. You could feel the whole building waiting. But it was as if he had forgotten how."

The Pistons repeated as NBA champs the next season, beating the Portland Trail Blazers in the Finals. Detroit was eager to make it three championships in a row, but it was not to be. For several years, the rugged Pistons had beaten up on the high-flying Chicago Bulls in the postseason. But in the 1991 playoffs, the Bulls finally won, ending the Pistons' glory days.

THE BADDEST BOY

During the years when the Detroit Pistons were known as the thuggish "Bad Boys," Bill Laimbeer was the worst of them all. He threw elbows, fists, and hips into his opponents whenever it served him. He probably earned more boos and awful nicknames from opposing fans than anyone in the history of the NBA. Opposing players hated him, too. Laimbeer was punched by the best of them: Robert Parish, Bob Lanier, Charles Barkley, Scottie Pippen, and Larry Bird. As Bird once said, "We don't like him that good." But despite all that, Laimbeer—a four-time All-Star—was a valuable player and was beloved in Detroit. He helped the Pistons to a pair of championships and became the 19th player in NBA history to collect more than 10,000 points and 10,000 rebounds.

PISTONS IN THE '90S

THE PISTONS STRUGGLED OVER THE NEXT FEW seasons despite maintaining the core of the team—Thomas, Laimbeer, Dumars, and Rodman. In 1992–93, the Pistons went 40–42 and missed the playoffs for the first time in 10 years. A year later, Rodman was traded to San Antonio, and Laimbeer and Thomas retired. After all of the changes, only Dumars remained from Detroit's championship era.

In the 1994 NBA Draft, Detroit began to rebuild by adding multitalented forward Grant Hill. Hill had a big impact on the NBA in his first season. The high-scoring rookie even led the league in All-Star voting, beating out Bulls superstar Michael Jordan. Helping him carry the Pistons were the ageless Dumars and strong young guard Allan Houston.

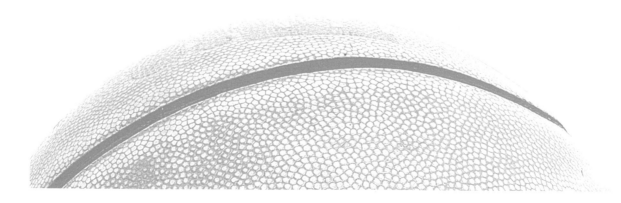

PISTONS

21

Allan Houston carved his name into the Pistons' record books by making 191 three-pointers in 1995-96

Jerry Stackhouse exploded for the best season of his career in 2000–01, scoring almost 30 points a game

Under new coach Doug Collins, the 1995–96 Pistons leaped to a 46–36 mark and a playoff berth. The Pistons brought in two key additions in 1997, trading for swingman Jerry Stackhouse and signing free agent center Brian Williams (who later changed his name to Bison Dele). Still, the team struggled for wins.

In 1999, Dumars retired and took a management position with the Pistons. Upon his retirement, the NBA created the Joe Dumars Trophy, which would be awarded each year to the player who best exemplified sportsmanship. Said league deputy commissioner Russ Granik, "Throughout his 14-year career, Joe carried himself with dignity and integrity and showed that one can be both a great athlete and a great sportsman."

In 2000, the Pistons lost their franchise player when Hill left town to join the Orlando Magic as a free agent. Rick Carlisle was inserted as head coach in 2001 and helped the Pistons reverse their fortunes. The next two years, Detroit finished 50–32 and built confidence with a number of playoff wins. Competitive basketball in the Motor City was back.

BISON DELE MYSTERY

Formerly named Brian Williams, center Bison Dele brought a sweet, left-handed shot and championship experience (with the Chicago Bulls) to the Pistons in 1997–98 and 1998–99. He was also an accomplished bass guitar player. But in 2002, Dele's brother, Miles Dabord, brought Dele's boat into a Tahiti port, arousing authorities' suspicions. Dele, his girlfriend, a skipper, and Dabord had been on the boat, but only Dabord returned. So what happened to Dele? Nobody knows for sure. Dabord, the main suspect and the only witness to the mystery, died before he could be interviewed. Some say Dele's boat was hijacked by pirates, but most assume that he and his girlfriend were killed and thrown overboard by Dabord, who was known to use his brother's identity to obtain money.

HOT

A rare all-around threat, forward Grant Hill earned All-Star status in five of his six seasons in Detroit

BASKET-BRAWL AT THE PALACE

When the Detroit Pistons took on the Indiana Pacers on November 19, 2004, at The Palace of Auburn Hills, no one expected a boxing match. But in this game, basketball would take a back seat to punching. As Pacers forward Ron Artest rested on the scorer's table after a scuffle with Pistons center Ben Wallace, a Pistons fan lobbed a drink that struck him. Artest jumped up into the crowd swinging his fists, and other Indiana players followed. A riot ensued as players and fans exchanged punches while ice, cups, and other debris rained down onto the court. After the brawl, many players were fined and suspended, and some fans were prosecuted. Said NBA Commissioner David Stern, "The events of the game were shocking, repulsive, and inexcusable, a humiliation for everyone associated with the NBA."

PISTONS STEAL A CROWN

BY THE 2003–04 SEASON, THE PISTONS WERE READY to challenge for a crown, boasting such players as defense-minded center Ben Wallace, smooth-scoring guard Richard Hamilton, tough point guard Chauncey Billups, and do-it-all forward Tayshaun Prince. Before the season, one of the NBA's most experienced coaches, Larry Brown, replaced Rick Carlisle as coach. The Pistons started the season well, but a midseason trade for volatile but talented power forward Rasheed Wallace kicked the Pistons into high gear. They finished 54–28 and raced through the playoffs to meet the Los Angeles Lakers in the NBA Finals.

27

PISTONS

Point guard Chauncey Billups's hard-nosed play on both ends of the court helped spark a Pistons revival.

NBA

At a long-armed 6-foot-9, Tayshaun Prince contributed both highlight-reel dunks and clutch blocks

The Lakers, fresh off three consecutive NBA championships from 2000 through 2002, featured four future Hall-of-Famers in center Shaquille O'Neal, guard Kobe Bryant, point guard Gary Payton, and forward Karl Malone—not to mention legendary coach Phil Jackson. But the Pistons shocked the experts by sweeping the Lakers in four straight games. "We didn't worry about what people wrote in the papers or what people were saying on TV," said Hamilton. "We said to ourselves, 'Anything is possible if you play together as five, not just on the offensive end but on the defensive end, too.'"

In 2004–05, the Pistons nearly pulled off a repeat. Relying on a lockdown defense, they marched all the way to the Finals before the San Antonio Spurs beat them, 81–74, in the deciding Game 7. Detroit seemed destined for a championship the following year after barreling to a franchise-best 64–18 record under new coach Flip Saunders. But the Pistons sputtered in the playoffs, losing to the Miami Heat in the 2006 Eastern Conference Finals. Still, they had accomplished much in just a few seasons. "We got to the Finals twice and won it once," said Billups. "I think that is a great run."

Getting back to the Finals soon is a doable goal in Detroit. The Pistons have always made their fans proud with their tough style of play, whether it was the "Bad Boys" or the current Pistons crew of defensive stalwarts. With the continued backing of the Detroit faithful, the Pistons will definitely keep the motor running.

BIG BEN With his own personal sound effect of a chiming bell, a fuzzy afro, and rippling arm muscles, 6-foot-9 Ben Wallace cut an imposing figure. His skill at defending the basket only added to the intimidation. Wallace was drafted by the Washington Bullets in 1996, but his career really took off when he joined the Pistons in 2000. After that, Wallace's individual accolades began to mount: three NBA Defensive Player of the Year trophies, top-three finishes in the NBA in rebounding and blocks for four straight years, and four selections to the All-Star team. But the Pistons' championship season of 2003–04 was what Wallace considered his finest accomplishment. "Yeah, [winning awards] means a lot, but it is not something I am going to hang my hat on," he said. "Winning the Finals is our main focus."

PISTONS

With four straight Conference Finals berths, the Pistons made the Palace of Auburn Hills a rocking arena